MIX
Papier aus verantwortungsvollen Quellen
Paper from responsible sources
FSC® C105338

Viktoria Schoja

Why Should Companies Invest in Social Media Marketing?

Parameters and Means for Performance Measurement

Anchor Academic
Publishing

Schoja, Viktoria: Why Should Companies Invest in Social Media Marketing? Parameters and Means for Performance Measurement, Hamburg, Anchor Academic Publishing 2016

Buch-ISBN: 978-3-96067-023-0
PDF-eBook-ISBN: 978-3-96067-523-5
Druck/Herstellung: Anchor Academic Publishing, Hamburg, 2016

Bibliografische Information der Deutschen Nationalbibliothek:
Die Deutsche Nationalbibliothek verzeichnet diese Publikation in der Deutschen Nationalbibliografie; detaillierte bibliografische Daten sind im Internet über http://dnb.d-nb.de abrufbar.

Bibliographical Information of the German National Library:
The German National Library lists this publication in the German National Bibliography. Detailed bibliographic data can be found at: http://dnb.d-nb.de

All rights reserved. This publication may not be reproduced, stored in a retrieval system or transmitted, in any form or by any means, electronic, mechanical, photocopying, recording or otherwise, without the prior permission of the publishers.

Das Werk einschließlich aller seiner Teile ist urheberrechtlich geschützt. Jede Verwertung außerhalb der Grenzen des Urheberrechtsgesetzes ist ohne Zustimmung des Verlages unzulässig und strafbar. Dies gilt insbesondere für Vervielfältigungen, Übersetzungen, Mikroverfilmungen und die Einspeicherung und Bearbeitung in elektronischen Systemen.

Die Wiedergabe von Gebrauchsnamen, Handelsnamen, Warenbezeichnungen usw. in diesem Werk berechtigt auch ohne besondere Kennzeichnung nicht zu der Annahme, dass solche Namen im Sinne der Warenzeichen- und Markenschutz-Gesetzgebung als frei zu betrachten wären und daher von jedermann benutzt werden dürften.

Die Informationen in diesem Werk wurden mit Sorgfalt erarbeitet. Dennoch können Fehler nicht vollständig ausgeschlossen werden und die Diplomica Verlag GmbH, die Autoren oder Übersetzer übernehmen keine juristische Verantwortung oder irgendeine Haftung für evtl. verbliebene fehlerhafte Angaben und deren Folgen.

Alle Rechte vorbehalten

© Anchor Academic Publishing, Imprint der Diplomica Verlag GmbH
Hermannstal 119k, 22119 Hamburg
http://www.diplomica-verlag.de, Hamburg 2016
Printed in Germany

Acknowledgements

Hereby, I wish to thank all people who in one way or another supported and guided me through my Master Thesis.

First of all I would like to thank to my supervisor, Prof. Dr. Nina Leffers, for her patience, understanding and guidance through all these months of writing.

I thank all professors and employees of the OTH Regensburg – Technical University of Applied Sciences of the last few years for their education and support activities.

Finally, I am grateful to my parents, my family and my close friends. Without their support, and their love, I would not be able to complete this project.

Table of contents

Acknowledgements 1

List of Figures 5

List of Abbreviations 6

Abstract 7

1. Introduction 8

    1.1 Social Media phenomenon 8

    1.2 Problem Statement 9

    1.3 Purpose 11

    1.4 Structure 11

2. Social Media and Marketing 12

    2.1 Social Media 12

        2.1.1 Definition 12

        2.1.2 Users 15

        2.1.3 Channels 16

        2.1.4 Communication 18

    2.2 Social Media Marketing 21

        2.2.1 Definition 21

        2.2.2 Traditional versus Social 23

        2.2.3 Marketingmix 25

        2.2.4 Strategies, Tactics, Practice 26

        2.2.5 Performance Measurement 29

        2.2.6 Monitoring 32

3 Social Media Channels 34

    3.1 Social Networks 34

        3.1.1 Facebook 35

- 3.1.2 Google+ 36
- 3.1.3 Snapchat 37
- 3.2 Professional Networks 38
- 3.2.1 XING 38
- 3.2.2 LinkedIn 39
- 3.3 Blogging & Micro Blogging 41
- 3.3.1 Weblogs 41
- 3.3.2 Micro Blogging Twitter 42
- 3.4 Content communities 43
- 3.4.1 YouTube – Video Sharing 44
- 3.4.2 SlideShare – Presentation Sharing 44
- 4. The Benefits and Challenges of Social Media 46
- 4.1 Brand awareness and customer acquisition 46
- 4.2 Customer Relation Management 46
- 4.3 Public Relations and Human Resources 47
- 5. Limitations and risks of Social Media Marketing 48
- 6. Conclusion & Outlook 50
- References 52
- Appendix 57

List of Figures

Figure 1: Flow of information in web 1.0 and web 2.0 12
Figure 2: Social Media 13
Figure 3: Social Media User Ladder 15
Figure 4: Social Media Channels 17
Figure 5: 1:1 media 18
Figure 6: 1:n media 18
Figure 7: n:n media 19
Figure 8: Online Marketing Areas 21
Figure 9: From a user to a customer 22
Figure 10: Bowling-Flipper-Theory 23
Figure 11: Conceptual Framework: Traditional versus Online Marketing Mix 25
Figure 12: Social Media Iceberg 26
Figure 13: Strategy for Social Media 27
Figure 14: Social Media Objectives 2011 28
Figure 15: Social Media Objectives 2012 28
Figure 16: ROI of Social Media 29
Figure 17: KPI's 30
Figure 18: Social Media Response Management Triage 33
Figure 19: Perception Gap 49

List of Abbreviations

Ibid. ibidem, "in the same place"

UGC User generated content

ROI Return on investment

KPI Key Performance Indicators

SEO Search engine optimization

CMS Content Management System

PR Public Relations

HR Human Resource

Abstract

Marketing has been impacted by social media and the internet developments. In the past decades there was a massive change within the disclosure landscape and the communication between the companies and their stakeholders. In order to stay competitive on the market, companies have to lighten up and identify advantages and opportunities given by social media.

This paper shows the motives for companies to invest in social media and clarified complicated concepts. Furthermore, it evaluates various social media channels and their effectiveness as well as return on investment measurements.

Using various social media platforms, companies benefit in different corporate areas, Marketing, Public Relations, Human Resource, or Customer Services. Since every platform has its own goals and approach different target audience, the companies has to choose the most appropriate platforms and develop a specific strategy.

To examine whether the objectives are achieved, performance measurement with its metrics are needed. Companies monitor the social media activities applying various tools as well as reviewing the Key Performance Indicators. Since the return on investment of social media is not quantifiable, companies examine the reach and user engagement and focus on building customer relations first, rather than selling the product, since a customer with a positive attitude towards the brand will more likely buy a product or service when needed.

Nowadays, it is essential for companies to be on social media to stay competitive and reach their target audience.

1. Introduction

1.1 Social Media phenomenon

The rise and wide spread of the internet let companies rethink their strategies and take into consideration a new ways of communication (Cheong and Morisson, 2008).

In less than three years the fastest growing online tool social media became the most popular activity on the web (Qualman, 2012). Social media can be explained as a new type of media. If Facebook were a country it would be the largest country in the world, with 1.49 billion monthly active users (Facebook Newsroom, 2015), followed by the population of China, 1.4 billion, and population of India, 1.28 billion (Worldometers, 2015). The usage of the internet became an inherent part in people's everyday life. Therefore, marketers should become aware of this great opportunity.

According to a BITCOM research an average internet user spend one quarter of their online time using social network channels like Facebook, Xing or Google+. Younger users cannot even differentiate between social media and the internet. An explanation to this could be, that 96 percent of the young internet users are members of at least one social network page and use internet generally for social media (Bitkom, 2012).

According to Qualman (2015), 92 percent of all companies state that social media is important for their business, which is an increase by 6 percent compared to 2013. A considerable number of companies use Social Media mostly for PR, HR, Marketing and Communication to drive sales, build traffic or find employees. However, some companies already took the next step to benefit from the strength of the online-communities using Open Innovation and Crowdsourcing to involve the consumer into the value creation process. Due to direct involvement the consumer establishes a deep emotional bond with the company which can increase brand awareness, loyalty, satisfaction, and convert the customer into a brand ambassador (Bitkom, 2013).

As Erik Qualman (2012) stated, "We don't have a choice on whether we do social media, the question is how well we do it". Companies that are deeply engaged in social media significantly surpass their competition in both revenues and profits (ibid.). If a company is not online and acts on the social media platforms, it gives the impression of being unimportant and not contemporary. According to Funk (2013), there are four key reason to get involved in social media:

- Target audience: 91 percent of online adults use social media. This is a big opportunity for companies to increase their market share and should not be ignored.
- Customer relationship: Social media gives a unique opportunity to build a personal connection with companies' brand loyalists.
- Word of mouth: Companies can let fans indirectly sell products by writing reviews, since 92 percent trust the recommendations of family, friends, and strangers.
- Competition: 88 percent of all businesses use social media for marketing purposes. Therefore, it is important to stay on track, since company's competitors are certainly among them.

Social media becomes an interesting field for investigation and investment. As Larry Weber (2009, p.283) says: "Social media is a new strategy that has the capacity of changing public opinion – every hour, minute, even a second. And why not changing customers brand attitude?"

1.2 Problem Statement

Social media has become one of the dominant forms of communication in the digital world, extremely changing the traditional relationship between a consumer and a business, since buyer behaviour has changed dramatically. It is the biggest shift since the industrial revolution. Where TV required 13 years to reach 50 Mio users, the internet only needed 4 years. An even faster development can be seen at the social media platform Facebook. With 200 million users in less than 12 months, Facebook make social media the number one activity on the web (Qualman, 2015).

When it comes to social media marketing, companies have to lighten up and literally fight for consumers' attention since the way corporations communicate and the way customers use the internet altered in the past ten years. Traditional marketing does not apply any longer, since the old concept of sender, the company, and receiver, the customer, is not applicable anymore.

Social media is the most influential source in consumer purchase decision. The majority of viewers, 86 percent, do not trust traditional advertising any longer and 90 percent do not respond to generic email or direct calls. The biggest drop can be seen within newspaper advertising which decreased by 18 percent where 24 out of 25 largest newspapers are experiencing record declines in circulation. While only 14 percent of customers trust ads, the majority, 76 percent, trust consumer recommendations for purchase decisions (Qualman, 2012). This is why companies have great opportunities in social media because of the worth of mouth or recommendations by other social media users.

Worth of mouth is common on social media; therefore, companies have to get customers to spread the message to each other to make it more genuine. There is no possibility for companies to buy attention, since "pay to play" does not apply anymore. Huge social media budget does not automatically mean success, as the marketer has to "play to play" creating authentic content which attract the customer (Quesenberry, 2015).

This issue is enhanced by the fact that customers are not only better informed but they are also busy and overworked due to the modern lifestyle and fast-moving environment. On social media platforms the customers are able to participate in every process of a product life cycle sharing their way of view with others in a timely basis.

The development of social media offers companies new opportunities and challenges to gain additional market share. By using social media companies can build trust and relationship to the customer. On the other hand, there is no border anymore and every company becomes transparent entering the world of social media and have to give a lot without expecting an immediate return. This is why it is so important for the companies to differentiate themselves from other companies on the social media if they want to stay competitive.

1.3 Purpose

The main purpose of this study is to obtain knowledge and emphasize the importance for companies to invest in social media marketing, as well as to investigate how they use it.

The research questions are:

1. Why is it important for companies to invest in social media?
2. How do companies use social media in their marketing communication?

1.4 Structure

The paper consists of two main parts – the theoretical part, using secondary data, and the case study, using primary and secondary data. It is subdivided into seven chapters with the following structure;

Chapter one introduces the topic and describes the social media phenomenon, followed by the problem statement, which declares the fast-moving issue marketers should be aware of. Next Chapter reflect the literature review. It introduces the concept of social media and all its' components, including the critically analysed relevant theories.

The Third chapter focuses on all significant social media channels, their use, advantages and disadvantages, as well as the performance measurements. Fourth chapter concentrate on the benefits and challenges of social media on special fields of application, followed by the limitations and risks the new media involve in chapter five.

Finally, chapter six concludes by summarizing the paper and providing an outlook on how social media will progress in the future.

2. Social Media and Marketing

2.1 Social Media

2.1.1 Definition

To understand the term Social media, it is essential to deal with the term web 1.0 and web 2.0 initially. While web 1.0 only focused on one-way communication, for example source of information, e-mail communication or e-commerce, web 2.0 integrate the user into the communication, Figure 1 (Bruhn, 2014, p.1036).

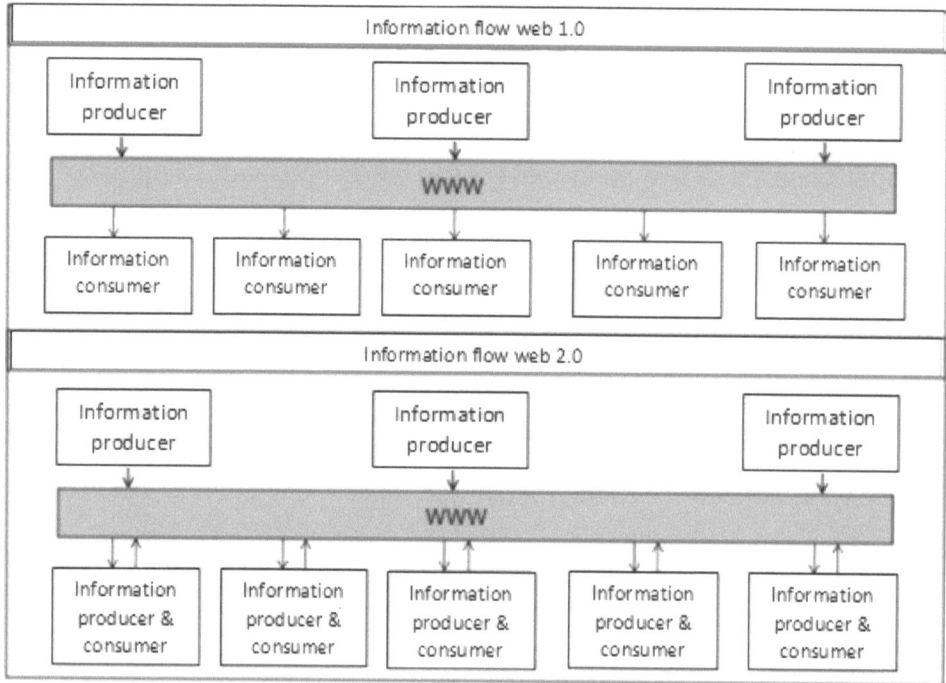

Figure 1: Flow of information in web 1.0 and web 2.0 (Bruhn, 2014, p.1036)

With web 2.0 users start to use the internet as a platform with user-generated content (UGC). It offers the user a possibility to create and share content on various platforms. Social media goes even further, since the users create, like, share and communicate the content to other users they have any kind of connection with, be it common friends, hobbies, shared interests. Therefore, the content gains social components (Grabs and Bannour, 2012). This UGC can be published as text, pictures, videos or audios (Hettler, 2010, p.14). Overall, users are able to build entirely new relationships online (Friedrichsen and Mühl-Benninghaus, 2013).

Kaplan and Haenlein (2010) describe social media as a group of web and mobile applications that build on the ideological and technological foundations of web 2.0 and it is used to turn interpersonal communication into interactive dialogue between organizations, communities, and individuals worldwide. This allows the creation and exchange of UGC to achieve social interaction and support idea sharing. Users are in control – as content consumers, as publishers and as influencers (Jordan Edmiston Group Inc., 2012).

There is a broad range of applications that can be used both by consumers and enterprises as shown in Figure 2. The implementation of these applications within a corporate environment is referred to as Enterprise 2.0 (Friedrichsen and Mühl-Benninghaus, 2013).

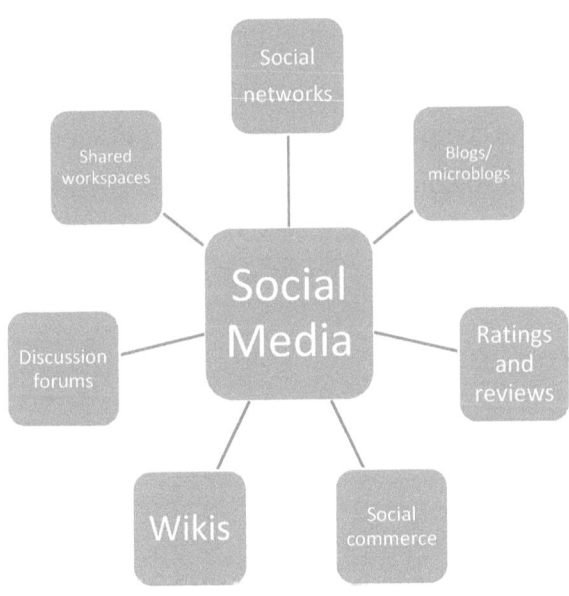

Figure 2: Social Media (Friedrichsen and Mühl-Benninghaus, 2013)

Mayfield (2008) defines social media as a new type of media which includes the sharing of opinions through blogging, microblogging, social networks, photo and video sharing websites, rating sites or company specific applications. It also includes characteristics, such as participation, openness, conversation, community and connectedness.

Social media covers many areas within a company, for example Marketing, PR, Sales, Customer Service or HR. The complexity, unknown area and all the possible fields of applications of social media lead to a new profession, Social

Media Manager. This person is responsible for monitoring and organization of the social media corporate performance (Düweke and Rabsch, 2012, p.155).

Through the use of social media companies are able to do businesses more effective at a very reasonable price with a higher range of coverage (Berthon, Pitt and Campbell, 2008). However, even it is effective, it does not mean that it has affected the consumer in the way company want. Consumers not only use social media for research or to share their content, however, they increasingly use it to engage with companies, by providing feedback and their own opinions (Garretson, 2008).

Corcoran (2009) complements an additional characteristic to social media and divides it into three types, owned media, paid media and earned media. Owned media is controlled by the company, for example the website. Paid media is bought by the company and includes online advertising, where earned media is not controlled by the company and includes word-of-mouth. Earned media is the media where social media marketing plays an important role, which will be discussed in 2.3.

2.1.2 Users

According to Grabs and Bannour (2012), there are five different types of users emerged from social media, Digital Natives, Digital Visitors, Digital Residents, Opinion Leaders, and Early Adaptors.

However, Forrester Research Inc. grouped consumers into six different categories of participation, visualized by a ladder, Figure 3.

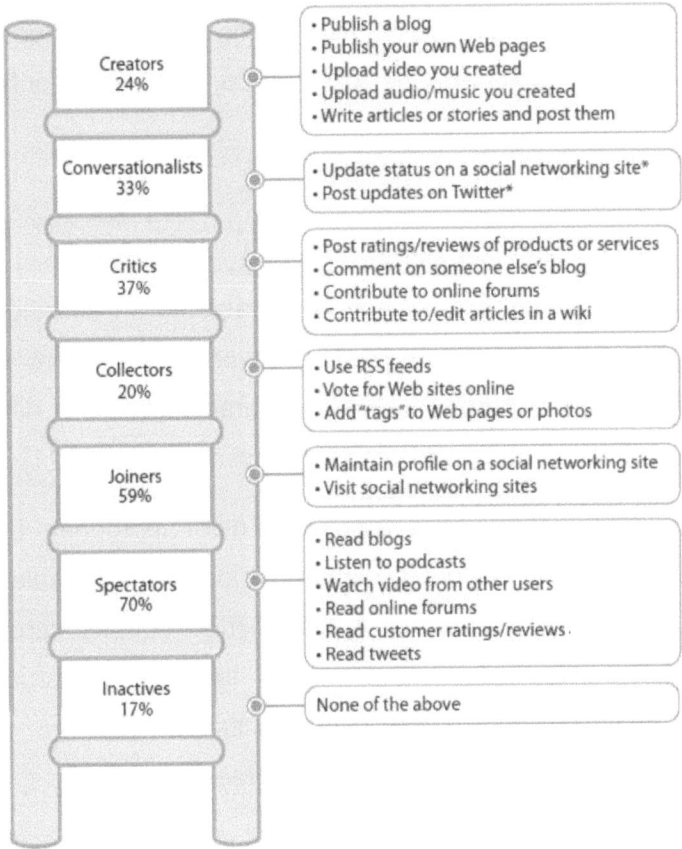

Figure 3: Social Media User Ladder (Forrester Research Inc., 2009)

The Inactives are not involved in any Social media activities. The major category, Spectators only observe, read, and watch the content on Social media. The second biggest category, Joiners, possess social networking profile, followed by Collectors, who organize the content for others. An important category for companies are the Critics, who respond to the content of others. Hence companies obtain direct feedback and benefit from it, since this feedback can be used for product developments. In the next category, Conversationalists, users actively share own opinions on Social media networking sites. The group with the highest participation rate, Creators, publish the social content consumed by others. It is here essential for a company to understand where the customers are located on the ladder, since the company can determine which strategy to use in order to reach those customers (Bernoff, 2010).

Recently, social media also gained in relevance for seniors. Therefore, almost all target groups exist on social media channels and can be reached by all kind of companies. At the moment 41 percent of people 65 years old and older are using social media applications (Bitkom, 2012). If this trend continuous, companies are able to approach an enormous target group, which is not online yet.

2.1.3 Channels

In current times, social media channels already have reached an enormous extent, as it can be seen in Appendix 'Social Media Conversations'. There are hundreds of applications and platforms with diverse characteristics that differ from each other in terms of functionality and scope (Kietzmann et al., 2011).

It is a significant challenge for companies to choose the most appropriate and effective application, where companies target audience is located, to be able to achieve the defined objectives. The use of social media requires careful analysis, planning, implementing and monitoring. If there is no proper application, the company should consider to establish its own platform, for example Fujifilm launched ZSpotNow.com (Kaplan and Haenlein, 2010).

To be successful companies should be present on more than one application and exploit the strengths of the different platforms. The advantages of application combinations go from cost saving to broader brand awareness. Should there be no possibility to maintain more than one channel, Funk (2013) recommend to be active on Facebook, as this platform captures 63 percent of all social media visits. Agreeing with this suggestion, Qualman (2015) adds another important application for marketers, LinkedIn, additional to Facebook. Appendix 'Active User', shows the main platforms with the most active users.

According to Grabs and Bannour (2012), "Friends, fans, and followers are the new term for virtual relationships between people. For companies it is important, therefore, to position themselves among their potential customers."

This work presents the most common and the most-used channels for businesses, Figure 4, which will be explained in detail in Chapter 3.

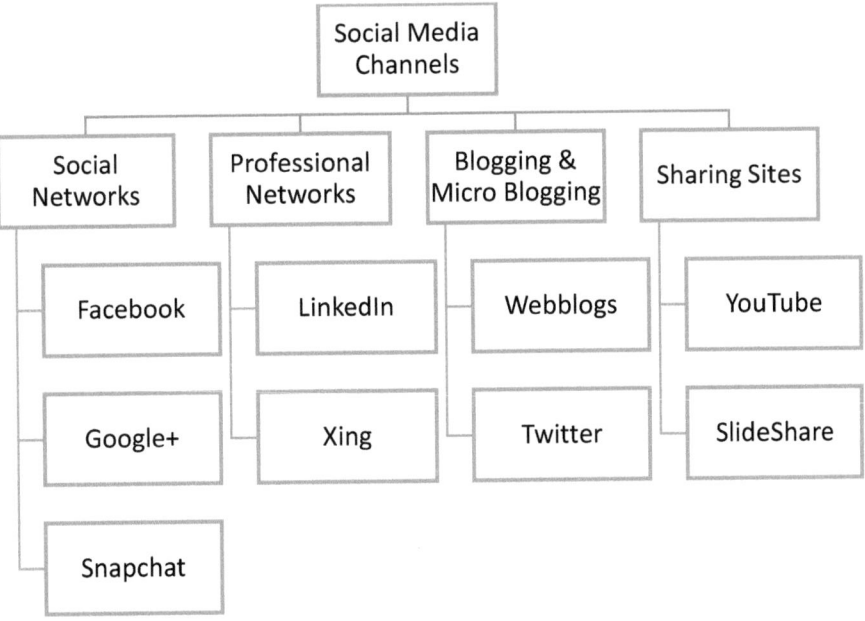

Figure 4: Social Media Channels (Own illustration)

2.1.4 Communication

Before social media existed traditional advertising via newspaper, TV, magazines or direct mail where the only way to communicate with the consumers, so called, 1:1 and 1:n media communication. 1:1 approach allow bilateral interpersonal communication where the content is intended for the two persons within the conversation only, Figure 5.

Figure 5: 1:1 media (Hettler, 2010, p.17)

1:n media communication enables the sender to deliver the message to many receivers. This communication strategy is generic for mass media like newspapers, TV, or radio, Figure 6.

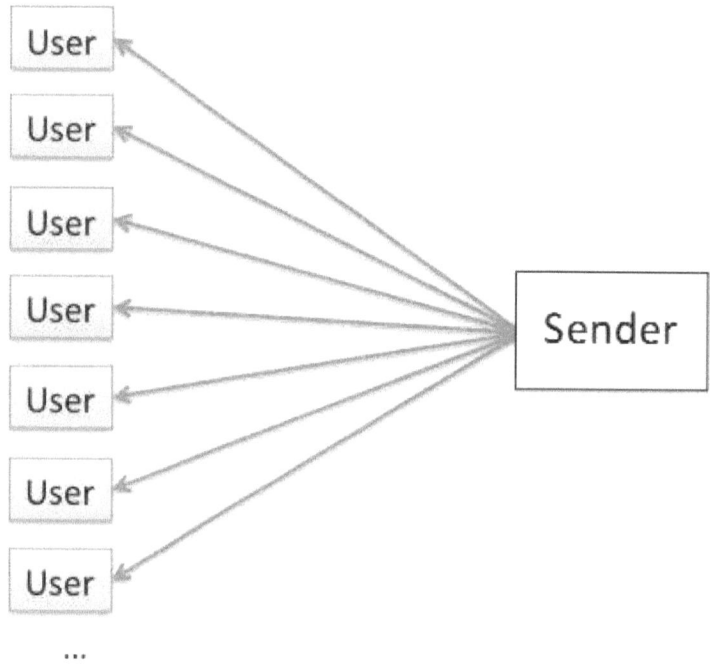

Figure 6: 1:n media (Hettler, 2010, p.17)

Social media creates a new form of communication, bidirectional n:n media communication, Figure 7. Here, many senders and users are able to communicate among each other and receive feedback straight away.

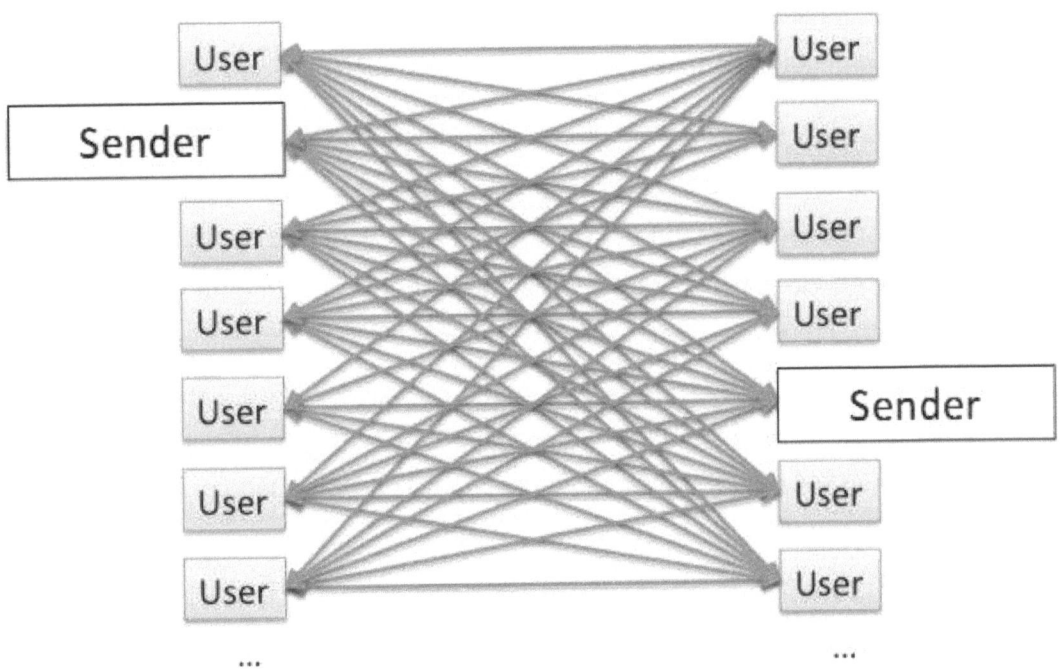

Figure 7: n:n media (Hettler, 2010, p.17)

There has been a shift from a one-to-many model to a many-to-many model. The traditional way of communication, 1:n, is not applicable anymore within social media, as the users are emancipated and do not accept to be receivers only. Social media provide users a possibility to create and exchange their own content and even achieve the same reach as traditional mass media (Hettler, 2010, p.17).

In relation corporate communication undergo a dramatic change lately. Companies that understand the new rules of marketing develop relationships directly with the consumers (Scott, 2010). Social media communication is all about the real-time, here and now. Users share, communicate, and criticize all incidents immediately. Therefore, it is vital for companies to monitor and react contemporary if any discrepancies or criticisms occur (Grabs and Bannour, 2012).

Traditional marketing used to use top-down-process by selling a product and applying the 4 P's of marketing, where the customers have no right of co-determination. Nevertheless, in social media the company first establish a customer relationship. If the customer is satisfied and convinced, then the company can sell the product (ibid). As Qualman (2015) stated: "News, products and services are not searched by people anymore. News, products and services will find and reach people via social media."

According to the Nielsen Study (2012), 92 percent of customers trust recommendations from people they know, while 70 percent trust opinions posted online from strangers. Only 47 percent trust the ads on TV or ads on radio, Appendix 'Trust'. Previously, in case of disappointments about a product or service, companies had to deal with dissatisfied and upset customers only, where nowadays those customers would spread the word using social media and call for boycott of the brand. Today customers can influence purchasing behaviour from others, which can be seen as a big advantage or a serious threat to a company (Grabs and Bannour, 2012).

Therefore, social media communication should not be isolated but integrated into the communication mix and linked with other media, such as TV, print, radio or banner. This combination is called crossmedia (ibid.). At the beginning of planning a campaign companies have to consider to integrate social media into the traditional media. An example is Haribo with their Fan Edition gummy bears advertising: a TV spot with a call to vote on Facebook or Haribo website for the favourite flavour, as the company launched fan edition gummi bears with flavours the customers have chosen.

Using crossmedia companies address a broad target group, along with an optimal distribution of the message. This enhance the probability to catch customers' attention with at least one media. Ideally the message will arrive to the customer on different channels. This evokes message repetitions and lead to an increased awareness.

2.2 Social Media Marketing

2.2.1 Definition

Besides the definition of social media, it is essential to understand how it is connected to Marketing. Social media marketing is a communication tool which is built on the social interaction of web 2.0 which breaks away from the traditional 1:1 communication and mass advertising (Hettler, 2010). Social media marketing is related to relationship marketing, where firms need to shift from "trying to sell" to "making connections with the consumers (Gordhamer, 2009).

Social media marketing is a completely new way of communication with the customer, and is using online communities, social networks, blogs and more to achieve own marketing goals (Hettler, 2012). According to the Bitcom research (2012), 72 percent of companies use this modern way of marketing.

It is not only about pushing out the message, but to create a two-way communication. Contrary to the traditional marketing the message is communicated in a softer, frank and human way. The message a company sends to the user becomes a part of the conversation, not an undesirable distraction.

Social media marketing is a part of online marketing, Figure 8 (Düweke and Rabsch, 2012). However, it should not be confused with online advertising and other online push marketing approaches, and should be implemented into the existing marketing, rather than being used as a replacement (Flagger, 2011).

Figure 8: Online Marketing Areas (Düweke and Rabsch, 2012)

In social media it is not suggestive to use push marketing, where companies attempt to take their products to the customer. Social media uses pull marketing, since the customers independently seeking for what matters for them. With regard to this fact companies have to provide information and answer any question the customers have, without assuming to sell the product in the first place (Grabs and Bannour, 2012). To address the customers' needs it is vital to empathize in the target person. Listening is becoming increasingly important, since social media marketing is speaking and listening, moving away from the traditional marketing monologue (Hettler, 2010, p.75).

If a company manage to convert a user into a customer, who talks about the product, write reviews and opinions and share it with his friends and followers, this consumer will become a brand ambassador through word of mouth, Figure 9.

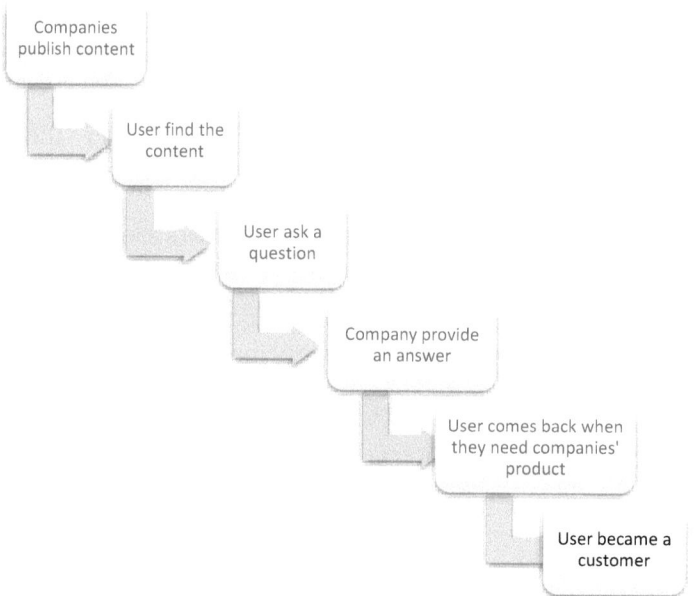

Figure 9: From a user to a customer (Grabs and Bannour, 2012)

2.2.2 Traditional versus Social

There is a big difference between traditional marketing and social media marketing, therefore it requires special consideration as the non-compliance leads to injury to reputation or failure. Where traditional marketing focus on single sales, volume and short-time timescales, social media marketing consider customer retention, customer value and long-term timescales. The main emphasis in the conventional marketing lies on product features and quality using TV, radio or print as a media. Against this the new way of marketing concentrate on relationship quality and customer service, taking advantages from social media channels (Friedrichsen, and Mühl-Benninghaus, 2013).

To simplify and understand the difference between traditional marketing and social media marketing, Thorsten Henning-Thurau (2012) developed a 'Bowling-Flipper-Theory', Figure 10.

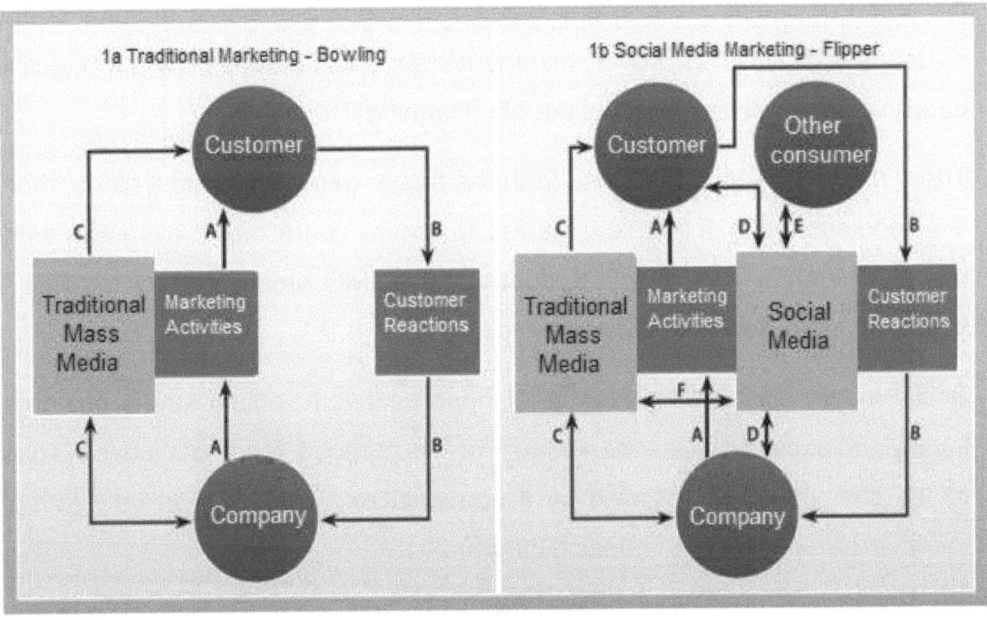

Figure 10: Bowling-Flipper-Theory (Thorsten Henning-Thurau, 2012)

Henning-Thurgau describes traditional marketing as a bowling game where the company tries to affect customers with its marketing activities (path A). If the marketing strategy is effective the customer buys the product or service (path B). Mass media officiate as mediator for the marketing content and PR (path C).

With social media there is a fundamental change in the theory since marketing is described as a Flipper game nowadays. The big change is that the customer does not only get affected by marketing activities but also act on social media channels, for example comment or evaluate a product, publish own YouTube video or share a product link with friends. The consequence can be both positive and negative with an enormous reach (path D).

The customers exchange own opinions with others, where they have the possibility to affect perceptions, preferences and behaviours (path E). Therefore, it is unpredictable whether the marketing effort will be advantageous or not, or even whether the company will suffer from a bad image or rise to the top.

Once there is a massive change, traditional media capture into the game (path F). The marketing messages swing between the two media models to increase the reach of people. This 'Highscore' for the company works as long as the message is positive. However, experience shows that especially the negative headlines increase the reach of people (Henning-Thurau, 2012).

There are two insights that arise from the flipper game. In the first place, there is an endless reach of people a marketing activity can achieve, even with a low budget. Secondly it is difficult to control the activity process and it requires a high level of sensibility and cleverness.

Social media offers companies great opportunities to obtain strong customer loyalty and expand affiliate marketing. For this purpose, a company has to listen to the customer first, followed by a conversation, which has to be informal, creative, personal and authentic (Ramge, 2015).

2.2.3 Marketingmix

Essentially everything a company attempts to do today involves the reach of social media, whether it is a promotion, a market research project, a recruiting, a product launch, a customer service or investor relations. From the viewpoint of a business one social media channel has many functions, since it might cover customer service, customer engagement and brand equity-building, promotion and customer retention all at the same time. Therefore, social media also belongs in the online marketing mix (Funk, 2013).

Compared to the traditional marketing mix, the online marketing mix contains another P, 'Participation', which stands above the 4 P's, Figure 11.

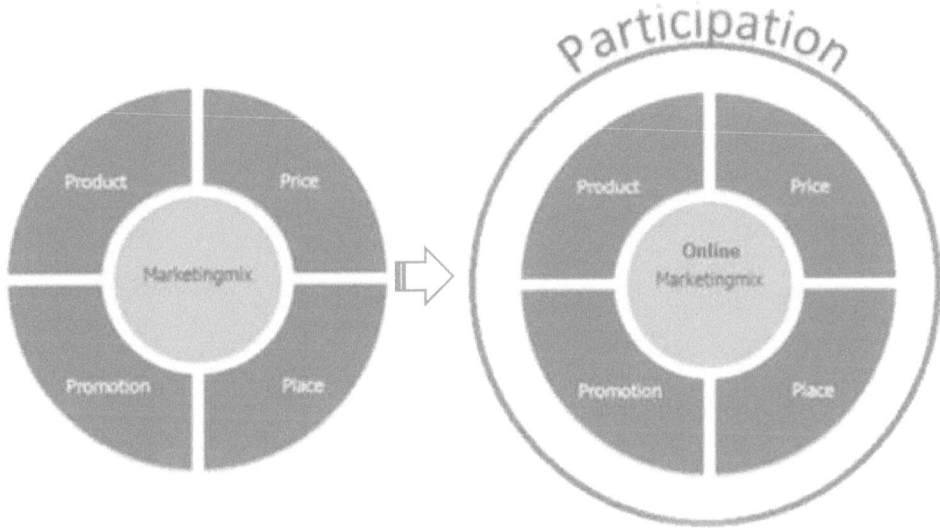

Figure 11: Conceptual Framework: Traditional versus Online Marketing Mix (Own illustration)

Participation is conducted by users and followers as they are involved in every single process. Social media tools can be applied in the production process, for example crowdsourcing, in the market research, for example social media monitoring, in sales, for example social commerce, or marketing communication, for example referral marketing. Thereby customers obtain the highest voice. No matter what the tool is being used for, it is always appropriate to approach your target audience first and sell the product eventually (Grabs and Bannour, 2012).

Social media is not only suitable for building up a customer relationship, but also for nurturing relations with shareholders and investors, as established trust is significant (ibid.).

2.2.4 Strategies, Tactics, Practice

To stay competitive in today's fast moving business landscape every social media marketing activity requires a conceived strategy. Whereby it is important to differentiate between strategies for social media and strategies for offline broadcast because that has shown to be one of the worst mistakes. It is essential for companies not only to see the peak of the social media iceberg, Figure 12, but to apply precise planning, consider every step, come up with new ideas, and be willing to take risks to stay competitive (Düweke and Rabsch, 2012, p.157).

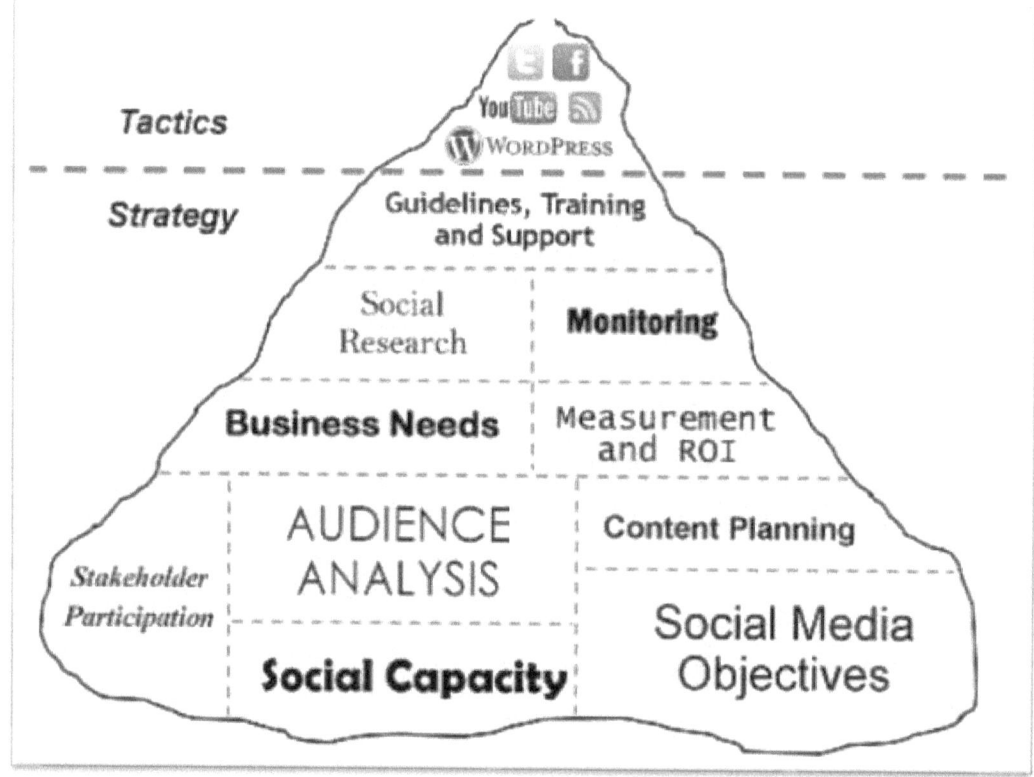

Figure 12: Social Media Iceberg (Düweke and Rabsch, 2012, p.157)

As stated by Schwarzenberger and Fantapie Altobelli (2012), Social media Strategic planning starts with objectives, Figure 13.

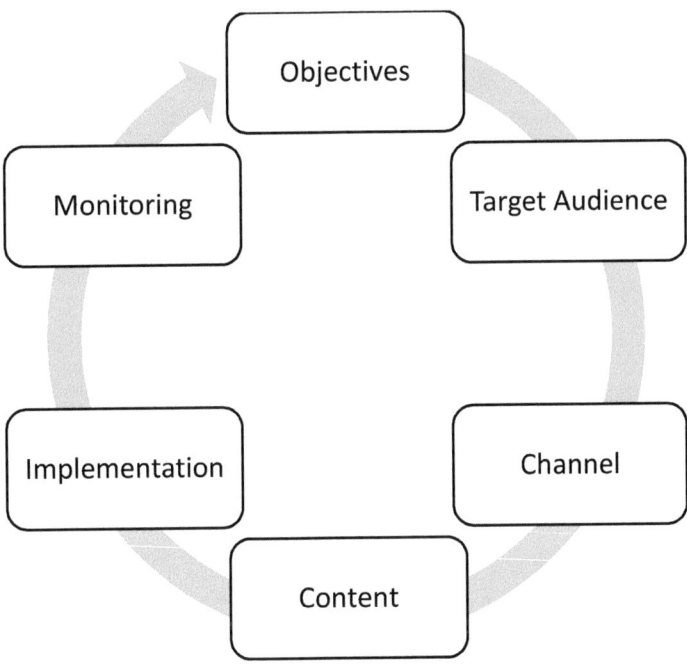

Figure 13: Strategy for Social Media (Schwarzenberger and Fantapie Altobelli, 2012)

It is essential to consider the target audience a company wants to address in order to choose the right channel and the right content. Afterwards the content has to be implemented on the chosen channel. As a final step it is vital to monitor whether the predefined goals are reached.

Charlene Li and Josh Bernoff, however, consider the POST framework as the right tool for the social media strategy. POST stands for People, Objectives, Strategy, and Technology. Compared with Schwarzenberger framework, POST framework change the process and looks at the target audience first before it derives objectives and formulate the strategies. Only in the last stage companies decide which social technologies to apply (Grabs and Bannour, 2012). Nevertheless, the POST framework does not consider monitoring, which is crucial for companies to examine whether the objectives are achieved.

There are two studies which examined the social media objectives companies set in 2011 (IBM, 2011) and 2012 (Bitkom, 2012), Figures 14 and 15. Detailed results can be found in Appendix 'Social media Objectives'.

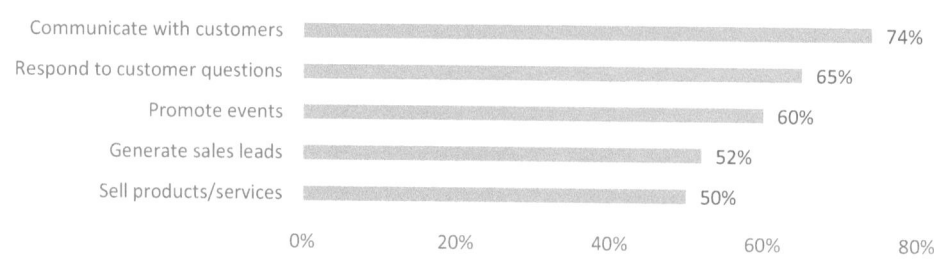

Figure 14: Social Media Objectives 2011 (IBM, 2011)

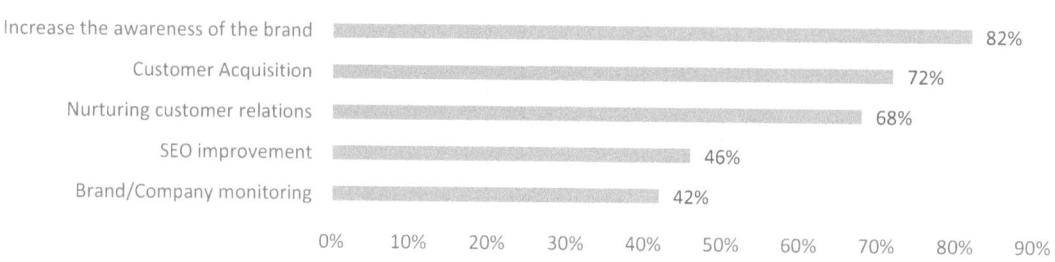

Figure 15: Social Media Objectives 2012 (Bitkom, 2012)

According to a BITCOM research in 2012 the most important Social media objective for companies was to increase brand awareness (82 percent), followed by customer acquisition (72 percent).

A detailed strategy guide for social media for businesses can be found in Appendix 'Quickstart'.

2.2.5 Performance Measurement

Social media marketing is able to bring a company the desired success, however, without figures it is challenging to measure the return on investment (ROI). There are four approaches for companies to measure the impact, Figure 16 (Funk, 2013).

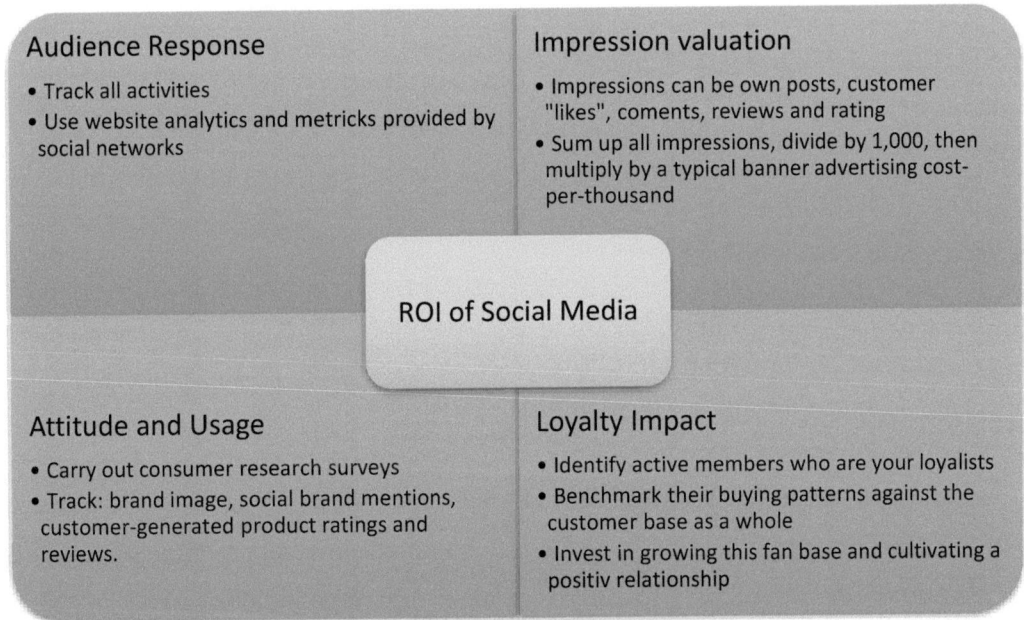

Figure 16: ROI of Social Media (Funk, 2013)

Not only the four approaches measure the ROI but also the cost savings. Companies can replace costly call-centres with cheaper social channels and constantly gain free feedback from online communities. Additionally, expensive business travels can be replaced with webinars or online-conferences (ibid.).

Lembke (2011) focus on seven Key Performance Indicators (KPI), in order to measure and control the objectives of all social media marketing activities, Figure 17.

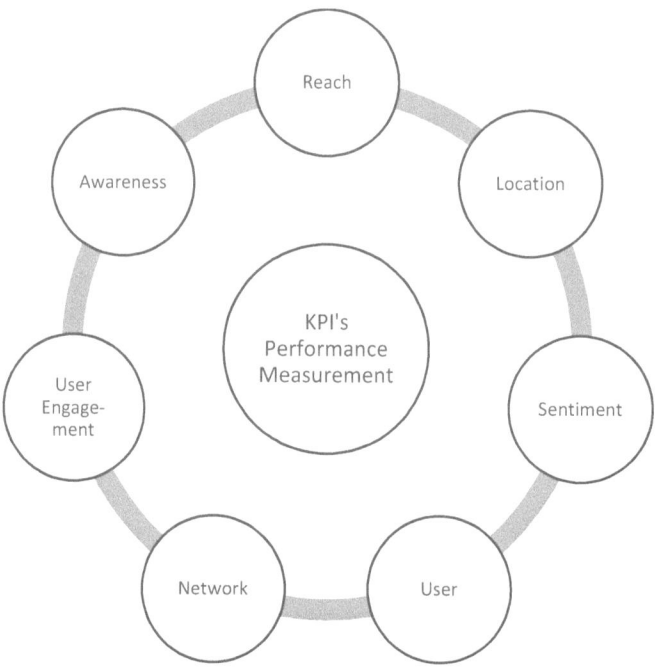

Figure 17: KPI's (Lembke, 2011)

Reach describes the scope of users an activity or a campaign is able to achieve. Location provide an overview of the relevant platforms, since not every channel is appropriate. Sentiment compares positive and negative conversations, which results the reputation of a company on social media. User differentiate between, Influencer, Authoritans, Connecter and Advocates. Those users are essential for a company since they are brand ambassadors. Network focus on the viral spread, for example when a fan shares a content. User Engagement describes the process on how the user deal with the content, whether the users watch it, share it, or provide feedback. Awareness is one of the most important indication for being successful on social media. This KPI correlates with User Engagement. A detailed description can be found in Appendix 'KPI Lembke'.

It depends on the company which KPI's to use, whether the company operate active or passive. According to Grabs and Bannour (2012) KPI's measure the conversation in the social web. Following KPI's can be used in social media:

- Share of Voice = brand mentions/total mentions (Brand + Competitor A, B, C, n…)
- Audience Engagement = Amount of comments + Shares + Likes/Amount of views

- Conversation Reach = Sum of all discussion participants / calculated discussion participants
- Active Advocates = Amount of active fans (last 30 days)/Sum of all fans
- Advocate Influence = Singular influence of fans / sum of all influences of fans
- Advocacy Impact = Amount of all fans initiated discussions/Sum of all fans
- Issue Resolution Rate = Amount of all successfully answered customer requests/ Sum of all customer service requests
- Resolution Time = Processing time for one customer request/ Sum of all customer service requests
- Satisfaction Score = Feedback (A, B, C, n…)/ Total feedback
- Topic Trends = Amount of all specific trend mentions/Amount of all topic trends
- Sentiment Ratio = (positive : neutral : negative brand mentions/Sum of all brand mentions
- Idea Impact = Sum of all positive comments, mentions, shares, likes/sum of all campaign discussions, mentions, shares, likes

The biggest threat of KPI is the fact that every conversation differs from another in terms of intensity and duration. However, social media cannot be ignored by companies, since ROI of social media is the "Risk of Ignoring" (ibid.)

Generally, "The ROI of Social media is – your business will still exist in 5 years" (Qualman, 2015).

2.2.6 Monitoring

Monitoring is an extremely important area of social media and describes the observation and control of comments and other UGC. Companies use it to observe user behaviour and to examine whether the social media marketing objectives are achieved. Social media monitoring is a continuous process and should be observed daily (Düweke, 2012).

Primarily, social media monitoring supports the company to figure out (Grabs and Bannour, 2012):

- Customer need
- Customer satisfaction characteristics
- Customer dissatisfaction characteristics
- How the user thinks about companies' competition
- New trends in company's specific sector

Many beneficial tools for monitoring are available online, Google Alerts, Social Mention, or How Sociable (ibid). It is advisable, especially for large corporation, popular brands and companies with international campaigns to use professional monitoring tools and work together with management consulting (Grabs and Bannour, 2012). No matter which monitoring tool a company uses, it should meet certain criteria (Lembke, 2011), all relevant platforms are covered; the company is able to look at specific countries only; possibility to refine a search with keywords; analysis time, how often does the company receives new information. Furthermore, it is essential to not rely on one tool only, but use various.

After the decision for the right monitor software, it is essential to know what to do with the provided results. In a case of a negative user reaction the company have to respond quickly to the situation to avoid bad publicity or even a shitstorm. A shitstorm describes a situation marked by violent controversy (Oxford Dictionaries, 2015), which can suddenly occur and spread far and wide on social media platforms. Social web demand a fast, but considered and professional response. To ensure this, companies can follow the Social Media Response Management Guide, Figure 18 (Brenner, 2011).

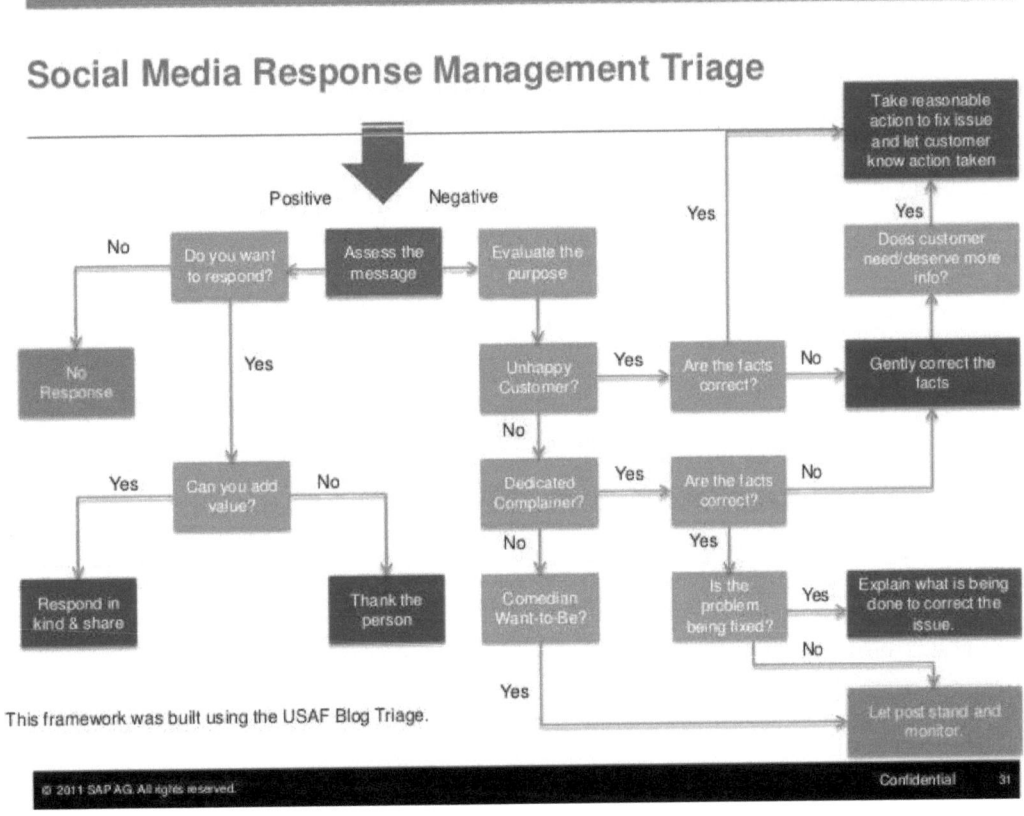

Figure 18: Social Media Response Management Triage (Brenner, 2011)

This response guide describes the most effective way of answering a positive or a negative comment or customer inquiry. If the message is negative, it definitely requires a response. In any way the response message, whether right or wrong, has to be gently and not aggressive. The user should not feel offended at any time. By providing response a company shows its sincerity and authenticity.

The company does not necessarily need to response to a positive comment, however this would show companies' engagement and the importance of the customer to the company.

3 Social Media Channels

3.1 Social Networks

Since their introduction in 1995 (Zarella, 2012), social networks have gained significant popularity and are among the most popular sites on social media. These days there are hundreds of social network sites, all representing different range of interests and practices.

According to Kaplan and Haenlein (2010), social networking sites allow users to create a personal profile on a specific platform and connect with others. Users can choose independently what content to share on their personal profile site, be it the real name, profile picture, age. "The presentation of a user's identity can often happen through the conscious or unconscious 'self-disclosure' of subjective information such as thoughts, feelings, likes, and dislikes" (Kietzmann et all, 2011, p. 243).

Social networks are web-based services that allow individuals to connect without geographical, political, cultural, or linguistic border. Therefore, the average number of Facebook friends is 350 per user. In the United States this number had been almost twice as high with 649 friends (Statista, 2015).

This is a great opportunity for companies to use this channel for word-of-mouth, since satisfied customers are the best multipliers and can spread the message rapidly. Moreover, companies can use social networks for market research, customer relationship, recruiting, or promotion (Grabs and Bannour, 2012).

There are various platforms to use, for the general masses, but also networks can focus on a specific lifestyle, topic or a location. It depends on the target audience which applications companies should use. This target audience can be found by mean of professional monitoring programs that shows where the potential customers exactly operate.

3.1.1 Facebook

First introduced in 2006, in the last view years Facebook developed into the largest social network, thus one of the most important platform for companies as it can be used for internal and external communication within a company (Huber, 2013).

Today, the platform has 1.4 billion users, making it the biggest platform online (Facebook, 2015). Companies are eligible to create an account on Facebook for free, and publish texts, videos, pictures, links, lotteries, or even start a survey using an available tool. According to Düweke (2012, P.183): "The new Pages helps businesses and organizations express their identity through features like cover photo and Page timeline. It also allows Pages to reach people on the web and mobile and respond to people in a quick, more personal way". Users can connect with any corporate Facebook page and become fans by "like" the page. Hence the user will see all posts on his wall from the specific company he liked.

When it comes to recommendation and sharing a corporate Facebook profile, the most essential aspect for the users are that the company regularly provide current and relevant content, a vibrant community and the individual address. On the other hand, users unlike a Facebook page if there is too much advertising and ignorance concerning any questions. (Grabs and Bannour, 2012). Thus, to be successful, companies should take the community and the individual user serious, and not consider them as an object only.

It is important to be active on Facebook and not underestimate the time and effort required to create, maintain and monitor the page, since it takes daily posting of engaging content that inspires interactions and maximizes reach (Funk, 2013).

Facebook is relevant for companies on many different levels. Since the platform exist worldwide, except China, it offers international companies an enormous opportunity for customer acquisition. The user reveals its own consumer behaviour, consciously or unconsciously, and provide the companies relevant information in order to reach the target audience more effective than ever more. Moreover, users not only use Facebook on a computer or laptop, but on mobile devices and tablets. This increase the period of time a company can get users' attention (Grabs and Bannour, 2012).

Facebook is suitable for extending the customer reach, forwarding the traffic to the own homepage, monitoring the activities and campaigns (ibid.). The fundamental metric in Facebook is the number of the fans following the company. Furthermore, Facebook provides demographic information of all fans by creating a clearly statistic (Zarella, 2012). Statistics help companies to improve the content quality and the overall performance (Grabs and Bannour, 2012).

3.1.2 Google+

Google+, a social network platform from Google, was first launched in 2011. User and companies can easily create a profile to connect and communicate with others. Other than on Facebook, Google+ does not have a certain pin board function, which means that a user is not able to post on other pages (Zarella, 2012). Nevertheless, commenting, sharing and like functionalities are available. A "like" on Facebook is called "+1" on Google+. This platform concentrate on the content, rather than on the connection, focusing on quality, originality and value in use (Huber, 2013).

Compared to other social networks, a great advantage of Google+ is the search engine optimization (SEO). All Google+ postings are indicated by the search engine and can be shown directly to the user. Therefore, it is essential for companies to have an account on Google+ to benefit from SEO (Zarella, 2012).

Google+ has an interesting feature, hangouts. This allow companies to video-chat with customers, colleagues or other users. Thereby, a company receives a direct feedback to its products or services, responses to customer inquiries, customer service or conducts any other customer-specific conversations. Currently not many companies use this great opportunity, however this is a rising trend, especially as many users use a smartphone for social media (Düweke, 2012).

There are no advertising options on Google+, as there are on Facebook, however, considering the fact and the advantages of SEO, Google+ offer free advertising, since the more information a company provide on the platform, the higher is the ranking within the search engine (Düweke, 2012). Therefore, companies using Google+ reach significantly extended target audience and improve local search visibility (Huber, 2013).

3.1.3 Snapchat

Snapchat was the fastest growing social network of 2014. Snapchat is a photo messaging application which was developed in 2011 (Bilton, 2012). It is a new way to take pictures or video adding text or drawings over a mobile phone and send them to friends or family with specifications on how long the photo will be available for viewing. User can set a time of 1 to 10 seconds for the viewing. The timer starts to count down the predefined seconds when the recipient opens the message. After the time is up the picture is deleted from the device and cannot be shown to the user anymore (Keller, 2012). Snapchat is a new way of sharing moments with friends on iPhone and Android.

Snapchat's marketing potential was published in September 2013. Brands can set up profiles on the network and add users as friends who opt into the brand's messages by accepting (Wong, 2013). Companies, for example McDonald's, provided their Snapchat fans 'behind the scene' exclusive photos from a TV launch of its new sandwich. In this way McDonald's engaged their fans to follow and improve brand loyalty (Reader, 2014).

Apps like Snapchat are quickly evolving from rapid messages between close friends to content-rich platforms that are open for brands to explore. In order to understand how to use Snapchat for marketing companies first need to understand their audience they are approaching. As a marketer Ryan Bonnici said, the app is interactive, therefore companies can create back-and-forth dialogue with followers in a way no other social media platform can.

The feature 'stories', which was introduced in 2013, was the main reason why companies are using Snapchat for marketing nowadays. As we live in a time where the attention is minimal the unique selling point of Snapchat is that the receiver pays attention while pressing and holding the screen as he or she knows that the snap will eventually disappear after the time run out. Snapchat stories is an extended feature as users are allowed to send a series of photos that last 24 hours.

Snapchat became a great opportunity for companies to drive businesses using brand specific content and reach particular target audiences through visual marketing. The purchasing power of Millennials is growing fast; therefore, Snapchat is the perfect intermediate link for brands.

3.2 Professional Networks

There are two main professional networks of a great importance for companies, XING and LinkedIn. Companies are able to create a corporate profile page, announce and promote important dates and events, create groups, lead discussions, look for new employees and place vacancies (Düweke, 2012). Primary function of professional networks is to connect to members you already know in real life (Zarella, 2012).

Other than the social networks, there are no photo galleries on professional networks. LinkedIn allow the user to upload a profile picture only. There is a basic membership available, but also a chargeable premium membership with more functions (ibid.). These aspects lead to a clear distinction between social and a professional networks and provide companies a distinct indication of seriousness along with transparency.

3.2.1 XING

XING is the most established professional network in Germany, first launched in 2003. There are two possibilities to connect with others on this platform, either to send a request to the person, or to introduce members among each other. XING support users to find fitting relations by an automated process (Zarella, 2012).

Companies using this platform gain various advantages in connecting, promoting, hiring and other functionalities. XING provides three different profile options for companies. The first option 'Standard' automatically listed the registered employees only. Second option 'Basis' additionally allow the company to add any company information and edit the employee list. Where the premium option "Plus" enable companies to update any corporate news and subscriptions (Zarella, 2012).

Companies with premium accounts are able to control the activities on XING with its intern monitoring tool. This tool records the traffic, detailed information about the visitors, for example, age, location, gender, the impact on marketing activities (Bester, 2012).

XING operates on the model of 'give and take', where companies provide useful information to others showing its competencies. Thereby users rank the company to a high level, which can be seen by other consumers. A top ranked company associates profitability and know-how (Grabs and Bannour, 2012).

3.2.2 LinkedIn

LinkedIn is the world's biggest professional networking site, with over 175 million members worldwide. This platform can be used for both, B2B and B2C. In case of B2B LinkedIn should be the centre of the corporate social media efforts. However, B2C business has also many valuable advantages using this platform, as it can help to build the brand image and connect with vendors, partners and potential employees (Funk, 2013).

The functionalities, structure and the benefits can be compared with those of XING. Companies can post or share distinguished information which signify them as an expert in their field and further their professional reputation. On LinkedIn user and companies can choose between free basic profiles and fee-based premium profiles (Düweke, 2013).

LinkedIn allow companies to create a corporate profile, which differ from a personal profile, since companies can publish information about the company and write articles. To be up-to-date companies can link their LinkedIn profiles to blogs, Twitter or Slideshare. Thereby, stakeholders can see a comprehensive picture of the company (Grabs and Bannour, 2012).

Additionally, groups on LinkedIn are vital for companies to provide support to other user and demonstrate competence. This is done my answering and commenting any group postings or writing own articles. Users evaluate company's contribution and award points. The more points the company has, the higher is the expert status shown on the corporate profile (ibid). Thereby, company establish itself as an opinion leader (Zarella, 2012).

Similar to XING, companies can look for new employees and place vacancies. The potential applicant receives a link to apply which lead to the corporate career site. Therefore, LinkedIn causes homepage traffic and in best case helps to find a qualified employee.

3.3 Blogging & Micro Blogging

When social media era begun, blogs were the first application to use. These applications allow user to publish short articles called posts (Zarella, 2010) and participate a multithreaded conversation online (Weber, 2009).

Blogging and Micro Blogging is the central place for interested customers. According to the earned media, companies share the information and the potential customers buy a product if they are convinced. Additionally, the comments in a blog can be used to receive direct and credible feedback.

3.3.1 Weblogs

Blogs were the first meaningful wave of social media (Funk, 2013). It can be compared to a personal online journal with the most recent entry first, and various features, for example tone, topic, links, comments and subscription (Mayfield, 2008). Zarella (2012), describes blogs as a sort of Content Management System (CMS), which can be used to publish short articles, first introduced in 1994.

Düweke (2013) differentiate between two types of blogs, public and intern. Corporate blogs are usually public blogs, however, companies can create their own intern blogs for employees only. This blogs can be used in specific projects for communication and discussions, as well as for team formation.

The author writes his blog usually in an informal way to show sincerity and authenticity. Moreover, it is vital to make references to other websites or other blogs. By doing so, the author increases the reach of other blogs as well as adding his own content more information. Generally, every blog contains a comments section, to give a reader the opportunity to provide feedback and interact with other users (Kaplan and Haenlein, 2010).

User generated blogs can be advantageous for companies. Positive written blogs create higher corporate reputation. On the other hand, negative blogs can easily destroy a good reputation of a company. Furthermore, companies are able to publish content with commenting functionality, so called Corporate Blogs. From a corporate prospective it is an inexpensive but an effective way to build the personal brand and directly connect to some like-minded internal and external stakeholders (Hettler, 2010). However, even corporate blogs should be conversational in tone, since it is not the right place for corporate-speak press releases (Wright, 2006). To increase the popularity of a blog, companies can publish a link to the blog on other social media platforms, mention the blog in the newsletter or direct mailing (Düweke, 2012). To monitor blogs companies can use various tool, for example PubSub or Technorati (Düweke, 2012).

3.3.2 Micro Blogging Twitter

Microblogging is a combination of blogs and social networks (Mayfield, 2008). The most popular application with the most users is Twitter, first introduced in 2009. The content of Twitter is called "tweets" and contains maximum 140 characters per message. Companies use Twitter to tweet about new content, offers, any news, or response to a question, since it is an easy, fast and cost-effective way (Zarella, 2012). Twitter, first introduced in 2006, is build up on blogs, however, with a short, clear text message without photos or videos. There is an option to publish a link which forward to other platforms, photos, videos or companies' homepage. 'Follower' are users who follows the company and the messages. 'Following' are all the user who are followed by the company (Grabs and Bannour, 2012).

Using hashtags "#" companies show the connection of the tweet to other topics or campaigns. By clicking on the hashtags, the user follows all messages which are related to the certain tag (Zarella, 2015). Great strength of Twitter is the real time communication. Where the users get the message before the media companies and newspaper publisher start writing an article. Since Twitter is mainly used in the United States, international companies should consider integrate Twitter into social media activities in order reach the target audience. To make proper use of Twitter companies can utilize a tool which filter tweets according to the determined keywords. This function will show only keyword relevant tweets and enables the company to save time (Grabs und Bannour, 2012).

Followers on Twitter represent the potential reach and determine the top-user-ranking. For marketing purposes, it is vital to gain as many followers as possible.

However, a company can obtain more followers by pursuing others and estimating them to follow the company in return. Not only the number of followers is important, but also the amount of retweets (Zarella, 2012). Retweets are comparable with shares on Facebook.

To measure the performance on Twitter, companies evaluate customer conversations. Some of the metrics are the mentions, amount of retweets or direct messages. If a company fulfil customer requirements or provide great customer service, the customers will usually publish a positive tweet. This action will establish a good reputation among the platform. Since Google indicates all published tweets, it is a great opportunity for a company to show presence on social media (Grabs and Bannour, 2012).

3.4 Content communities

Content communities include applications, where users can upload and share their own videos, pictures, presentations, or any other user-generated content. There are communities for pictures, Instagram, for videos, YouTube, or for presentations, SlideShare (Kaplan and Haenlein, 2009). YouTube is particular suitable for marketing (Bruhn, 2014).

Users share daily millions of information in content communities, according to 'We are what we share'. In conclusion, companies share not only the content but the company's value, corporate philosophy and their point of view. The more a company shares, the more it convinces customers to choose this particular product (Grabs and Bannour, 2012).

Content communities offer companies innumerable advantages. It can extend the reach, since users share interesting content, enhance SEO ranking, pulls traffic to the homepage, provide a cost-effective tool to develop own website, as the content can be published there (ibid.)

The most important metric for content communities is the amount of viewings of photos, videos or presentations. Since it is a social media sharing site the amount of comments, subscriptions, followers or likes, are vital measurements as well (Zarella, 2012).

3.4.1 YouTube – Video Sharing

YouTube, first launched in 2005, is the biggest video sharing portal with community-functionality. It enables the user, called 'subscribers', to watch, share, integrate, or even create and upload own videos. In addition, there is a possibility to transfer the videos to other social media platforms (Hettler, 2010).

Companies hope their videos to go viral. However, even small success stories, fun and relevant videos, can connect with the target audience. YouTube can benefit the brand image and boost search-engine visibility (Funk, 2013).

To achieve high reach, companies should try to appear on the 'top videos' – list. In order to do this, it is essential not only to publish the video, but also to share it on other platforms, to enhance the visibility (Zarella, 2012).

Compared to a Facebook post or tweet, watching a video is a much longer period of time. Thereby the subscriber deal with the content more effective, since there is almost no possibility to be engaged otherwise. The shorter the video the more engaged are the audience, since the human attention span is limited (Zarella, 2012).

YouTube provides a monitoring tool, YouTube-Insights, for every single video. This tool provides important information regarding the development of the video performance, focusing on a specific time frame, as well as the demographic data to the users who watched the video. Using this data, a company can figure out areas to improve and optimize the sharing functionalities (Grabs and Bannour, 2012).

3.4.2 SlideShare – Presentation Sharing

In the recent time, there was a boom within the presentation sharing platforms with the most popular one, Slideshare. Similar to YouTube, Slideshare allow users to follow other users or companies and download the content with permission. Within various working areas, for example, consulting, marketing, or PR presentations play a significant role, since this is the first impression of professionality and competence of the presenter and shows the effort behind the work (Grabs and Bannour, 2012).

While uploading data it is essential to use necessary keywords in the headline as well as in the description. Not only presentations are in demand but also manuals, instructions or corporate statistics. However, include references to copyrights in every content which will be published. Using a fee-based corporate account, companies are able to link up to three conferences where they gave lectures (Zarnella, 2012).

A company can show its professional content to other users and connect to the community at the same time. Providing relevant high-quality content increases the visibility and the reach of companies' level of expertise additionally to enhanced SEO (Grabs and Bannour, 2012).

4. The Benefits and Challenges of Social Media

4.1 Brand awareness and customer acquisition

With only one click on the "like"-button the user shows on average to 130 Facebook-friends that he likes the company, a special product or a corporate activity. Facebook fans of a brand spend twice as much as those who are not Facebook fans. 74 percent of consumers who interact with the company through social media have a more positive brand impression (Funk, 2013).

Never before it was easier to suggest an information to another person or even cause a viral effect. Now, with Social media it is possible to increase the range of the brand and the message more efficient and more effective, especially if a company already located its 'influencer' (Grabs and Bannour, 2012). Social media platforms turn into branding mechanisms by directly communicating their brand value among consumers (Pencak, 2011).

Social media is the most reliable and promising method of reaching new customers (Weber, 2009).

4.2 Customer Relation Management

Social media benefits can not only be found in branding and customer acquisition but also in interactive communication, between company and customers or among customers. Web 2.0 has shifted customer service dramatically converting it into customer service 2.0 (Funk, 2013).

If a customer receives a competent customer service on social media, this user will tell three times as many people about it as a nonuser of social media. McKinsey Global Institute estimates that the better communication, achieved through social media, could add $1.3 trillion to the global economy (ibid.).

Social media has made it simpler and significantly more cost-effective to keep in touch with existing customers, to inform about the company and any news, as well as to provide customer service. Although a company receives negative customer feedback, it can be perfectly used for improvements, product developments, and innovations. This valuable feedback is an open brainstorming for businesses (Grabs and Bannour, 2012). Previously, if a customer had question, an issue or a concern, the only way to get an answer was to call or write an e-mail. In current times, however, they increasingly use social media.

On the other hand, it is one of the key challenges to integrate social media into customer relation management. The consumer has become more powerful than ever with social media, gaining the control to make or ruin a campaign, product, service, or even the whole brand (Funk, 2013).

4.3 Public Relations and Human Resources

Besides the change within the way of communication there is a shift in Public Relations (PR), from the traditional mass media to online communication. The shift of the PR-Activities to online channels simplifies the data exchange. Press releases can be send feaster to a wide range of journalists. Due to Web 2.0 and Social media there are way more information than ever before. Journalists does not only depend on corporate statements but they can also use UGC published in blogs, forums, communities, own expectations and own experiences. This content is not whitewashed and implicate a high value of information (Hettler, 2010, p.33).

Today, everyone can be a journalist, since people around the world post and publish relevant content in real time. However, this is a big threat, since there is no overview anymore whether the content is real, current or credible.

In current times, 89 percent of companies use social media for recruitment, via LinkedIn, Xing, Facebook, and other country-specific applications (Qualman, 2015).

This is a great opportunity for companies, since the social media communities are of enormous size. In the past, candidates could only search for a position on company's website or at career fairs, however this limit the opportunities for both, the potential employee as well as the hiring company. Hiring company reach many more jobseeker on social media platforms and can review the candidate profile, which is much more cost-effective.

5. Limitations and risks of Social Media Marketing

The bright sight of social media, nonetheless, has limitations and risks. The ever-changing environment force companies to be flexible and prepared to take risks.

To develop an effective strategy, it requires time investment as well as skilled personnel. Since companies hardly provide social media budget, there is lack of possibilities to involve and maintain the new media.

As the consumer became more powerful an increase in user-generated complaints can be observed, but many companies, especially retailers, have issues to deal with negative ratings. However, this is one of the most important steps, since the consumer want to be taken seriously (Udayan-Chiechi, 2015). A response to both, positive or negative comments, should be transparent, which shows the consumer the corporate sincerity. A beneficial response guide can be found in Figure 19: Social Media Response Management Triage. Companies can adapt and use this in order to be prepared, especially in case of bad publicity.

Companies which do not use social media base their decision on the fact that the target audience their approach are not present online, for example pensioners. Another reason against the use of social media are legal uncertainty, for example data protection law or copyright (Bitkom, 2012).

Another risk is 'Facebook Fatigue'. This phenomenon describes the loss of young people on Facebook. The reasons for this are the more attractive applications, like Snapchat or WhatsApp. Additionally, the aggressive advertising is responsible for Facebook Fatigue, as well as the fact that increasingly older people use this platform. As young people do not wish to be friends on Facebook with parents or other relatives, they avoid using it (Financial Times, 2013).

With 642 million active users there is a big market, China, where Facebook, Twitter and Co are blocked. Companies who trade in China have to shift to other alternative platforms. Sina Weibo, a microblogging platform accounts 25 percent of all active users as well as QZone, a social network, with the same percentage (We are Social, 2015).

Additionally, there is a perception gap between consumer view and companies view, Figure 19 (IBM, 2011).

Figure 19: Perception Gap (IBM, 2011)

Companies have some misperceptions regarding why consumers interact with them via social sites. The main reasons for customers to be online are to get discounts and purchase products or services they had reviewed. On the other hand, companies think that customers are online because they want to learn about new products and obtain general information or write reviews on product and services they already used. This Figure shows the challenges companies have to overcome in future. To achieve this it demands better listening to the customer and the requirements.

6. Conclusion & Outlook

For companies there is no excuse for not having a strong presence on social media, no matter if it is a small business or a global company. Using social media companies learn the new way of doing businesses and not only use social media for promotion, since there is way far more behind. They understand the new rules of marketing develop relationships directly with the consumers.

Social media is all about connection, ideas and information sharing, engaging meaningful dialogues, but first of all about listening. The rules of social media are simple to follow since it contains participation, connection, conversation, community and listening to the market place.

Every single social media platform has its own features and characteristics. It depends on the company, what exactly this company wants to achieve. Whether to broaden the reach, provide the best customer service or to hire employees, every company should consider the consumer as brand ambassadors who spread the word of mouth virally.

Companies have to recognize the shift in the communication and the way marketing works today. Away from the traditional marketing towards the social web marketing. However, it is essential to use crossmedia and combine both marketing ways in order to be efficient in today fast-moving environment. Users' participation stands above the 4 P's, as described in the conceptual framework, and is included in every single sector which provide companies great opportunities to increase the reach and obtain customer feedback.

The answer to the question of why it is important for companies to invest in social media is simple: To survive and stay competitive in nowadays business, it is essential to follow the consumers, to listen to the consumers and provide information without expecting anything in return. If the consumers are satisfied with companies' overall performance, they will come back when they need the product or service. Building a strong customer loyalty is essential in social media, since the competition is there as well.

Another important aspect is the monitoring and performance measurements, companies have to recognize and adapt, according to their specific needs. This tools provide customer insights and show areas to improve.

In the future the mobile use will gain in importance, since users want always to be available. This is a significant aspect for companies, since the communication will become even more important for companies. They will have to adapt and develop strategies according to this change.

There is an alternative way arises, how to advertise to the target audience, using SMART TV adapted tools. Since every SMART TV have an internet connection, users connecting their social media activities with TV. Thereby, using certain tools companies are able to send an advertising with an adopted content to the special target person. This way a customer who 'likes' cats on Facebook, will be targeted with a cat food advertising while watching his favourite movie on the TV. Consumers as well as the companies has become transparent in today's business world.

References

Books and Articles

Bitkom (2012) Social Media in deutschen Unternehmen. p.6-28

Bitkom (2013) Presseinformation. Social-Media im Unternehmenseinsatz. p.1-2

Bruhn, M. (2014) Unternehmens- und Marketingkommunikation, 3rd Ed. München: Vahlen.

Cheong, H., and Morrison, M. (2008). Consumers' reliance on product information and recommendations found in UGC. Journal of Interactive Advertising, 8(2), p.1-29.

Düweke, E. and Rabsch, S. (2012) Erfolgreiche Websites. 2nd Ed. Bonn: Galileo Computing.

Friedrichsen, M. and Mühl-Benninghaus, W. (2013) Handbook of Social Media Management. Berlin: Springer.

Funk, T. (2013) Advanced Social Media Marketing, How to lead, launch, and manage a successful social media program. New York: Apress.

Grabs, A. and Bannour, K. P. (2012) Follow Me! Bonn: Galileo Computing.

Hettler, U. (2010) Social Media Marketing: Marketing mit Blogs, Sozialen Netzwerken und weiteren Anwendungen des Web 2.0. Oldenburg: Oldenbourg Wissenschaftsverlag.

Huber, M. (2013) Kommunikation und Social Media, 3rd Ed. München: UVK

Lembke, C. (2011) Social Media Marketing. Berlin: Cornelsen

Qualman, E. (2012) Socialnomics. How social media transform the way we live and do business. 2nd Ed. Westford: Courier Westford.

Quesenberry, K. A. (2015) Social Media Strategy. Marketing and Advertising in the Consumer Revolution. Lanham: Rowman & Littlefield.

Schwarzenberger, M. and Fantapié Altobelli, C. (2012) Social Media Strategien. Entwicklung und Implementierung mittels einer Social Media Scorecard. Institut für Marketing, p.6.

Weber, L. (2009) Marketing to the Social Web. New Jersey: John Wiley & Sons.

Scott D.M. (2010) The new rules of marketing & PR – how to use social media, blogs, new releases, online video, and viral marketing to reach buyers directly. 2nd Ed. New York: John Wiley & Sons, Inc.

Wright, D.K. and Hinson, M.D. (2006) How blogs are changing employee communication: Strategic questions for corporate public relations. Paper presented to the Public Relations Society of America International Conference, Salt Lake City Utah

Zarella, D. (2012) Das Social Media Marketing Buch, 2nd Ed. Köln: O'Reilly, Köln

Online

Bernoff, J. (2010) Social Technographics: Conversationalists get onto the ladder. [Online] Available from: http://forrester.typepad.com/groundswell/2010/01/conversationalists-get-onto-the-ladder.html. [Accessed: 10th Sep 2015].

Berthon, P., Pitt, L. and Campbell C. (2008) When customers create adds, California Management Review. [Online] 50, (4), 6-30. Available from: http://www.researchgate.net/publication/237011492_Ad_Lib_When_Customers_Create_the_Ad. [Accessed: 10th Sep 2015].

Bester, M. (2012) XING blog. Erfolgsmessung leicht gemacht. [Online] Available from: https://blog.xing.com/2012/04/erfolgsmessung-leicht-gemacht-statistiken-im-unternehmensprofil-plus-und-noch-viel-mehr/. [Accessed: 30 Aug 2015].

Bilton, N. (2012) Disruptions: Indiscreet Photos, Glimpsed Then Gone. [Online] Available from: http://bits.blogs.nytimes.com/2012/05/06/disruptions-indiscreet-photos-glimpsed-then-gone/. [Accessed: 30 June 2015].

Brenner M. (2011) SAP. Integration Social Media into the B2B marketingmix. [Online] Available from: http://de.slideshare.net/michaelbrenner/integrate-social-media-into-your-markcting-ix. [Accessed: 10th Sep 2015].

Corcoran, S. (2009) Defining owned, earned, and paid media. [Online] Available from: http://blogs.forrester.com/interactive_marketing/2009/12/defining-earned-owned-and-paid-media.html. [Accessed: 10th Sep 2015].

Ethority (2015) Social Media Conversations. [Online] Available from: http://ethority.de/social-media-prisma/. [Accessed: 22 Aug 2015].

Facebook Newsroom. (2015) Company Info. Stats. [Online] Available from: http://newsroom.fb.com/company-info/. [Accessed: 15th Sept 2015].

Financial Times (2013) Facebook fatigue' stirs investor concern. [Online] Available from: http://www.ft.com/intl/cms/s/0/8b7ab90e-bc91-11e2-b344-00144feab7de.html. [Accessed: 22 Sept 2015].

Flagler, R. (2011) Are you social? Marketing your business with Facebook and Twitter. [Online] New York Amsterdam News; 7/7/2011, Vol. 102 Issue 27, pS.6. Available from: http://connection.ebscohost.com/c/articles/63149762/are-you-social-marketing-your-business-facebook-twitter. [Accessed: 20th Aug 2015].

Garretson, R. (2008) Future tense: The global CMO. [Online] Available from: http://graphics.eiu.com/upload/Google percent20Text.pdf. [Accessed: 10th Sep 2015].

Gordhamer, S (2009) 4 Ways Social Media is Changing Business. [Online] Available from: http://mashable.com/2009/09/22/social-media-business/#XSVotenDxkk_. [Accessed: 20th Aug 2015].

Henning-Thurau, T. et al. (2012) Flipper statt Bowling – Marketing im Zeitalter von Social Media, [Online] Marketing Review St.Gallen. Available from: http://www.villiger-marketing.ch/images/news/Flippern-statt-Bowling.pdf. [Accessed: 20th May 2015].

IBM (2011) From social media to Social CRM - Part II. [Online] Available from: http://www-01.ibm.com/common/ssi/cgi-bin/ssialias?infotype=PM&subtype=XB&appname=GBSE_GB_TI_USEN&htmlfid=GBE03416USEN&attachment=GBE03416USEN.PDF. [Accessed: 10th Aug 2015].

Jordan Edmiston Group Inc. (2012) The Social Media Ecosystem. [Online] IAB Database. Available from: http://www.iab.net/media/file/JEGIIABSocialMediaReport.pdf. [Accessed: 10th Sep 2015].

Kaplan, A.M. and Haenlein, M. (2010) Users of the world, unite! The challenges and opportunities of Social Media [Online] Business Horizons, Vol. 53 (2010), S. 59-68 Available from http://www.sciencedirect.com/science/article/pii/S0007681309001232. [Accessed: 20th Aug 2015].

Keller, J. and Bloomberg (2012) Facebook's Poke Is a Wild Success—for Rival Snapchat. [Online] Available from: http://www.businessweek.com/articles/2012-12-28/facebooks-poke-is-a-wild-success-for-rival-snapchat. [Accessed: 30 June 2015].

Kietzmann, J. et al. (2011) Social Media? Get Serious! Understanding the functional building blocks of social media. [Online] Business Horizons, 54, 241-251 Available from: http://www.sciencedirect.com/science/article/pii/S0007681311000061. [Accessed: 20th Aug 2015].

Mayfield, A. (2008) What is Social Media. [Online] V1.4 Update. Available from: http://www.repromax.com/docs/113/854427515.pdf. [Accessed: 10th Sep 2015].

Nielsen (2012) Consumer trust in online, social and mobile advertising grows. [Online] Available from: http://www.nielsen.com/us/en/insights/news/2012/consumer-trust-in-online-social-and-mobile-advertising-grows.html. [Accessed: 20th Aug 2015].

Oxford Dictionaries (2015) Definition. [Online] Available from: http://www.oxforddictionaries.com/definition/english/shitstorm. [Accessed: 10th Sept 2015].

Pencak, S. (2011) How to brand for effective marketing. [Online] Available from: https://wejungo.wordpress.com/tag/silvia-pencak/. [Accessed: 30 Aug 2015].

Qualman, E. (2015) Social Media Revolution 2015. [Online] Available from: http://www.socialnomics.net/2015/01/26/social-media-revolution-2015/. [Accessed: 10th June 2015].

Ramge, T. (2015) Flipper statt Bowling. [Online] Brandeins 02/2015. Available from: http://www.brandeins.de/archiv/2015/marketing/wie-funktioniert-gutes-marketing-flipper-statt-bowling/. [Accessed: 20th May 2015].

Reader, A. (2014) Brands experiment with Snapchat to reach and engage millennials. [Online] Available from: http://www.theguardian.com/media-network/media-network-blog/2014/aug/21/snapchat-brands-marketing-lynx-mcdonalds-southampton-fc. [Accessed: 30 Aug 2015].

Statista (2015) Durchschnittliche Anzahl von Facebook-Freunden bei US-amerikanischen Nutzern nach Altersgruppe im Jahr 2014. [Online] Available from: http://de.statista.com/statistik/daten/studie/325772/umfrage/durchschnittliche-anzahl-von-facebook-freunden-in-den-usa-nach-altersgruppe/. [Accessed: 10th Sept 2015].

Udayan-Chiechi, P. (2015) Nur authentische Marken setzen sich durch. [Online] Available from: https://www.adzine.de/2015/01/nur-authentische-marken-setzen-sich-durch-social-media-marketing/. [Accessed: 30 Aug 2015].

We are Social (2015) Top active social Platforms. China. [Online] Available from: http://was-sg.wascdn.net/wp-content/uploads/2015/01/Slide1001.png. [Accessed: 22 Sept 2015].

Wong, D. (2013) Snapchat Marketing Is Now a Thing. [Online] Available from: https://www.outmarket.com/snapchat-marketing/?utm_source=feedburner&utm_medium=email&utm_campaign=Feed percent3A+VocusBlog+ percent28Vocus+Blog percent29 [Accessed: 30 June 2015].

Worldometers. (2015) Current world population. [Online] Available from: http://www.worldometers.info/world-population/#top20. [Accessed: 15th Sept 2015].

Appendix

Social Media Conversations

[1]

---

[1] Ethority (2015)

Quickstart

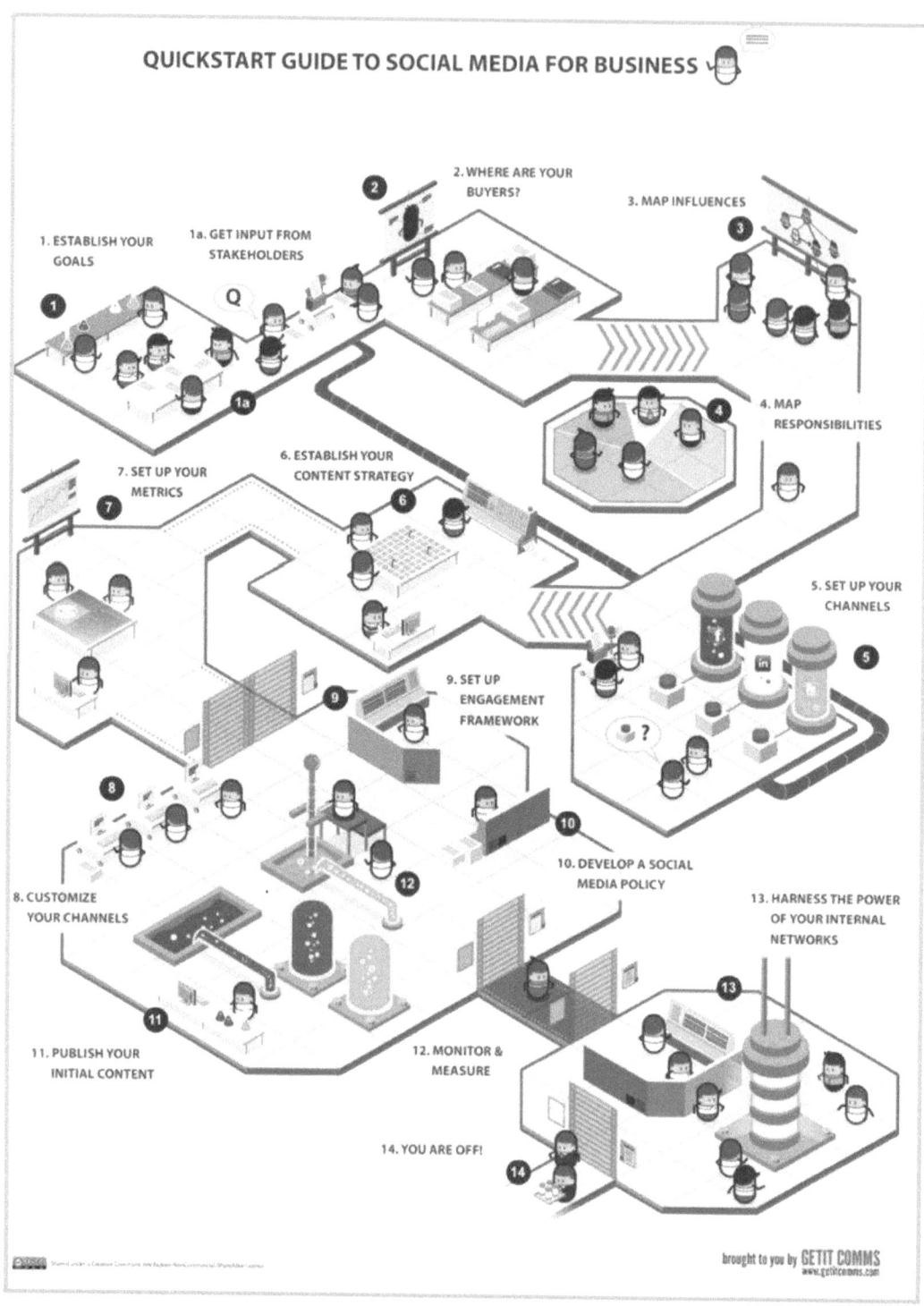

Trust

To what extent do you trust the following forms of advertising?

Global Average	Trust Completely/Somewhat	Don't Trust Much/At All
Recommendations from people I know	92%	8%
Consumer opinions posted online	70%	30%
Editorial content such as newspaper articles	58%	42%
Branded Websites	58%	42%
Emails I signed up for	50%	50%
Ads on TV	47%	53%
Brand sponsorships	47%	53%
Ads in magazines	47%	53%
Billboards and other outdoor advertising	47%	53%
Ads in newspapers	46%	54%
Ads on radio	42%	58%
Ads before movies	41%	59%
TV program product placements	40%	60%
Ads served in search engine results	40%	60%
Online video ads	36%	64%
Ads on social networks	36%	64%
Online banner ads	33%	67%
Display ads on mobile devices	33%	67%
Text ads on mobile phones	29%	71%

Source: Nielsen Global Trust in Advertising Survey, Q3 2011

[3]

---

[3] Nielsen, 2012

Social Media Objectives

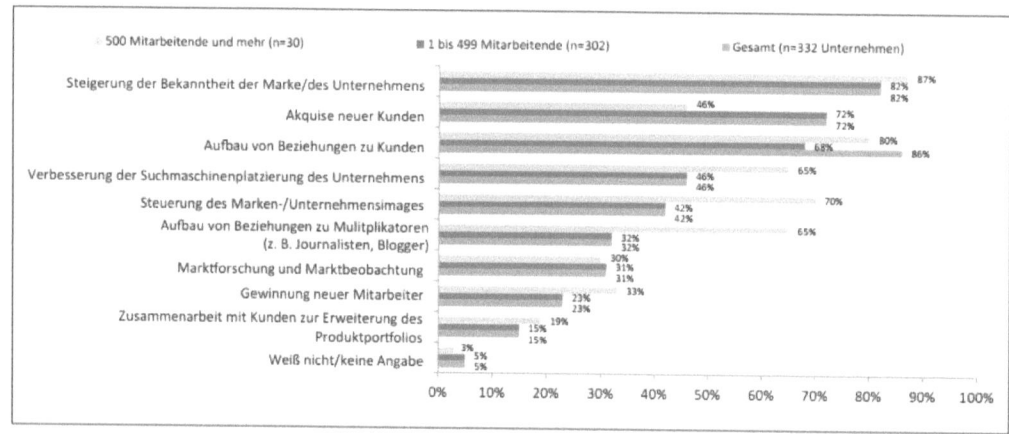

Schaubild III-J-13: Ziele von Social Media-Aktivitäten – Studie Bitkom (Bitkom 2012a)

[4]

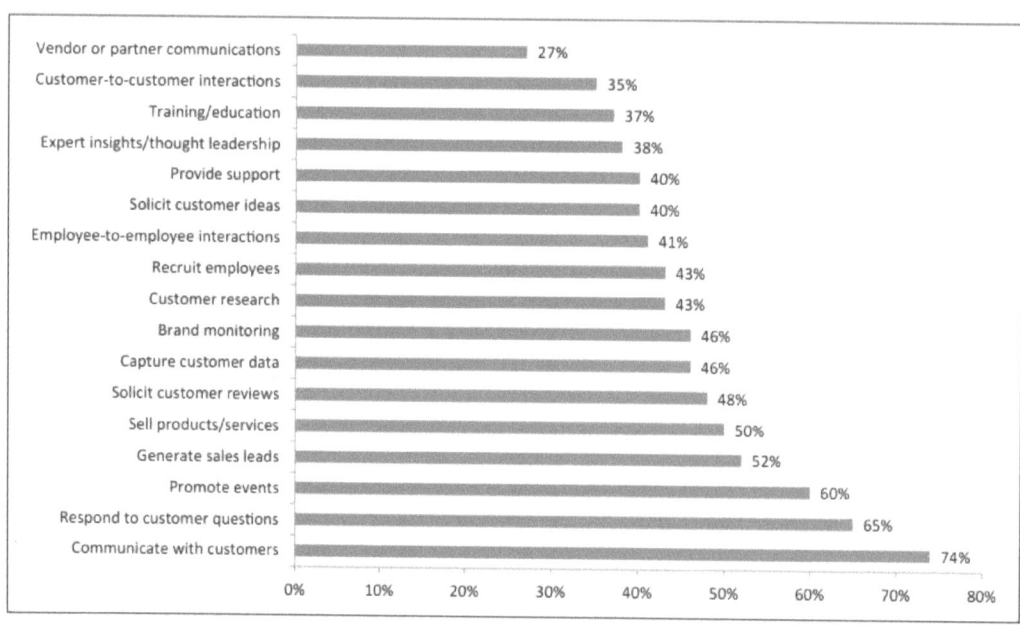

Schaubild III-J-14: Ziele von Social Media-Aktivitäten – Studie IBM (IBM 2011)

[5]

---

[4] Bitkom, 2012
[5] IMB, 2011

Active User

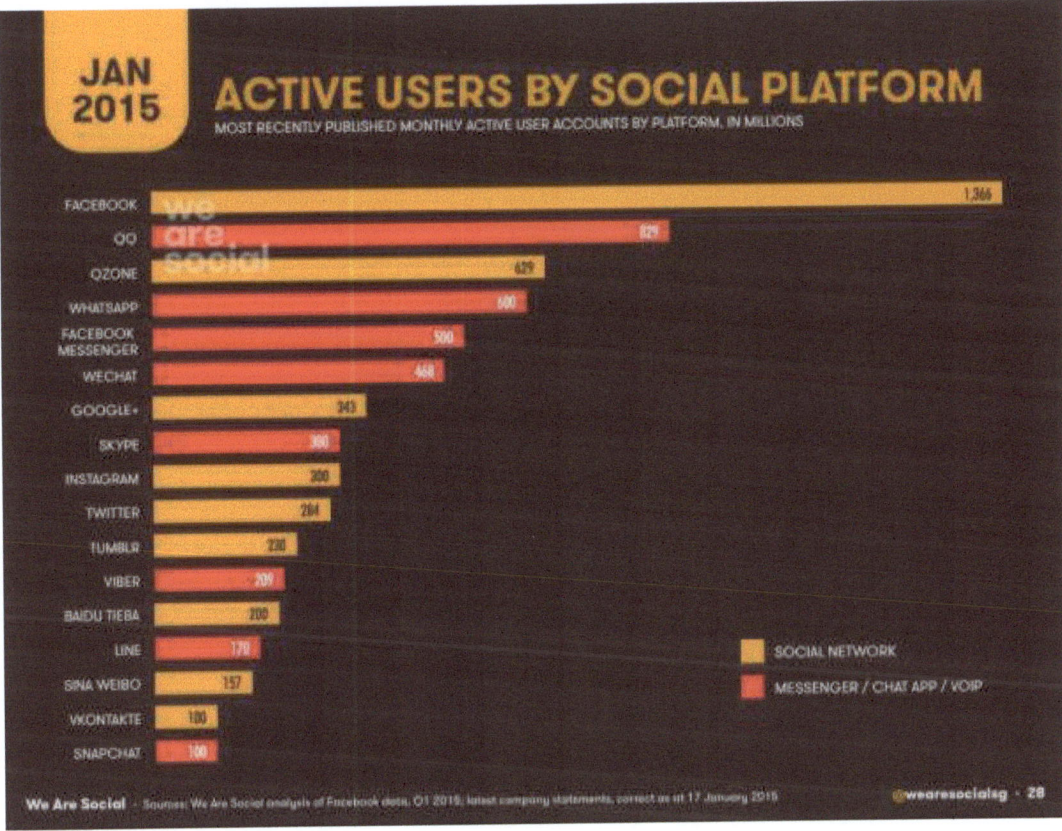

[6] We are Social, 2015

KPI Lembke

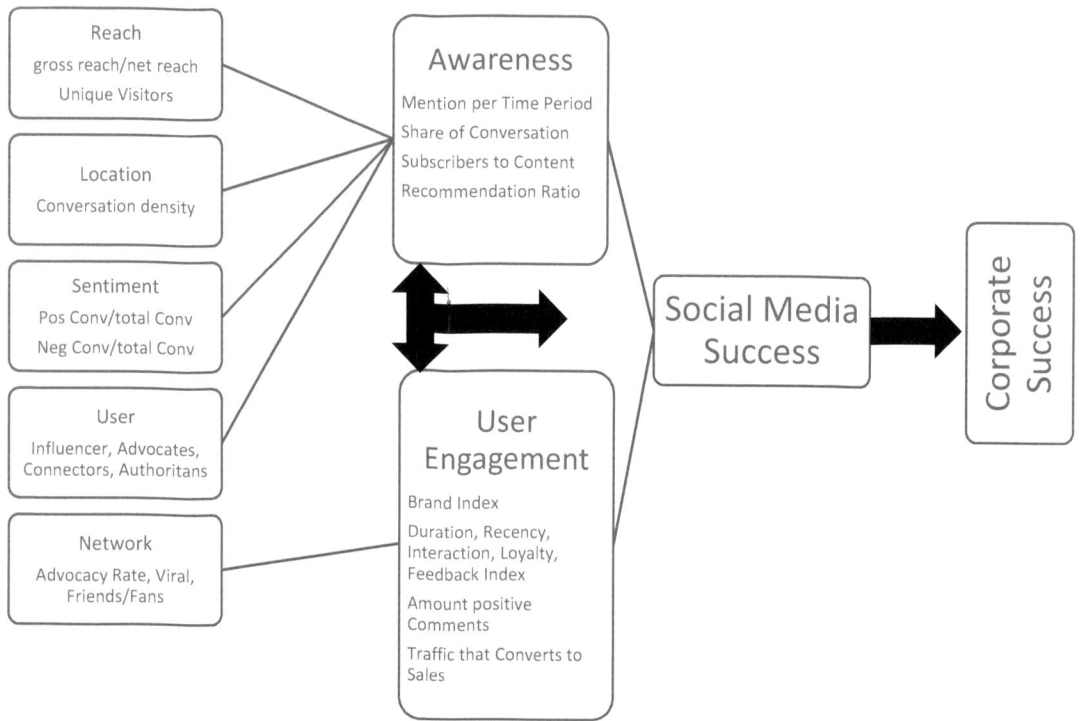

[7] Lembke, 2011